HELP! THERE'S A TEEN IN MY HOUSE

Six Secrets to Understanding Your Teen

Dina Comer

Red Town Publishing

Cape Coral, FL

Help! There's a Teen in My House
© 2013 Dina Comer

Red Town Publishing
Cape Coral, FL

ISBN: 978-1-940243-02-3

Library of Congress Control Number: 2013912487

Unless otherwise indicated, all Scripture quotations are taken from the Holy Bible, New International Version® *NIV® Copyright © 1973, 1978, 1984, 2011 by Biblica, Inc.® Used by permission. All rights reserved worldwide.*

Scripture quotations marked *(NLT) are from the Holy Bible. New Living Translation copyright© 1996, 2004, 2007 by Tyndale House Foundation. Used by permission of Tyndale House Publishers Inc., Carol Stream, Illinois 60188. All rights reserved.*

DEDICATION

This book is dedicated to my amazing husband, David, who has been a great role model for our kids and who has enjoyed the journey of parenting two wonderful children alongside me. This book is also dedicated to our two wonderful children, Joshua and Hannah, who have allowed us to see the pages of this book become a reality and who have made our lives so rich.

TABLE OF CONTENTS

FOREWORD

I've met hundreds of thousands of Christian leaders in my life, but very, very few female leaders of the caliber of Dina Comer. That's why you are going to smile very broadly that you picked up this book, *Help! There's a Teen in My House.* As you read the following pages, you will be reading far more than "just another book." You will be reading the essence and fiber of Dina's most important ministry—that of raising her amazing children.

Through my years in youth ministry, I've often reminded teenagers that their parents were often "just kids who grew up and had kids." How tragic, but true. Teenagers sure don't come with an attached "instruction manual." And busy parents often put far more effort into training for their careers and for their favorite sports than they invest into training for parenthood. *But you, my friend, must be different.* After all, you're about to read this engaging and practical book. Smart move. This puts you in a league of your own. Congratulations for not leaving the world of parenting a teenager on autopilot (unfortunately, the attitude many parents seem to adopt).

Dina parallels teenagers to Play-Doh throughout her chapters. Don't you remember that amazing stuff from your childhood? I sure do. It was messy but so very fun... moldable but easily broken when dry...and full of potential but in serious need of shaping. This is a pretty accurate version of teenagers in most anyone's book! But the principles behind Dina's chapters are far more than creative parallels to Play-Doh. She pours out her very life on these pages and allows us to journey with her. She has raised some amazing teenagers in the Comer household.

Lastly, allow me to share my heart with you about Dina herself, as my friend and as a respected lady of the Lord. Just get around her and you will quickly see why she has so captured my heart. She radiates warmth, authenticity, and joy in a way that is rarely seen 24/7. It's almost impossible not to be captured by the contagious love and passion she so genuinely extends to most everyone she meets. She and her husband pastor a thriving church. But in the midst of doing ministry, she has consistently lived out the statement: *"My main ministry doesn't begin when I drive OUT of the driveway in the mornings. Instead, it begins when I drive INTO my driveway when my family comes home."* Dina has balanced the world of ministry leadership: senior pastor's wife, youth pastor, and a hundred other roles; the most strategic ones of being a godly wife and raising her children. From my vantage point, she has done an A+ job.

So go get a good cup of coffee, find a comfortable chair, and enjoy this amazing book. You will be challenged, inspired, and motivated. Most of all, you will be reminded that there is no role on earth more important than that of raising some amazing teenagers. I can't think of a much higher calling. Nor can I think of a commitment that will ripple with more positive fruit when you enter eternity.

Cheering for you,
Jeanne Mayo,
Youth speaker, leadership coach, and author

PREFACE

I always enjoyed playing with Play-Doh when I was a kid. I especially loved squeezing each colorful ball of fun between my fingers and watching it ooze out the other side. Really, I'm not a gross person by any stretch of the imagination. It just seemed cool, having something pressed between my little fingers and then watching it come out the other side.

Of course, I loved all the things you could do with Play-Doh. (Nowadays, there are even more exciting possibilities!) When my children were old enough to start playing with Play-Doh, I was so excited to introduce it to them. I just knew they would have a blast with it, especially with all the gadgets that came with it. Talk about fun!

My family didn't have a lot of money when I was growing up, so I didn't have many toys. I can honestly say the ones I did have I really appreciated. I could hardly stand to wait when a birthday or Christmas would roll around, anxiously anticipating the new present I would receive. I'm not really sure which special occasion it was when I got my first "set of cans," but I do remember thinking of the incredible potential before me to mold some wonderful creations. Today, I just happen to view molding teens the very same way I viewed molding Play-Doh.

I believe teens and Play-Doh actually have quite a bit in common. In fact, there is much to learn by comparing teens to Play-Doh. After working with teens for well over twenty years now, and being the parent of two now grown teens, I happen to know you can mold your teen.

Over these two decades I've worked with teens, hopefully I've gotten a little wiser as I've grown older. I've worked with all sorts of teenagers: happy ones, sad ones, lonely ones, confused ones, abused ones, smart ones, not-so-smart ones (nicer way of putting it), pretty ones, not-so-pretty ones—the list goes on and on. I can assure you from my experience: shaping young people isn't a lost cause once they reach a certain age.

It cracks me up how people react after I tell them what I do for a living. They ask and I tell them without hesitation, "I work with teenagers—I'm a youth pastor!" The typical response I get is a pat on the back and the words: "Whew! I don't know how you work with *those* people." (Let's face it. Everyone who lives up to the age of twenty has experienced their very own exciting, yet often very scary teen years.) While I do believe that the teen years can hold some challenges, I also believe that the teen years can be some of the most exciting and important years of a person's life. I absolutely love helping "those people" walk through their ever-so-tender teen years.

If you've picked up this book, it's most likely because there's a teen in your house. So, how do you move past the mindset that the teen years are difficult to parent through or that teens cannot be molded? And if they are moldable, how do you mold teens correctly? My hope is that you will find the answers to these questions and more in the pages of this book.

In fact, I believe that parenting through the teen years will seem much more attainable as you learn the secrets to understanding your teen. So allow me to help you discover these secrets by showing you what teens and Play-Doh have in common.

INTRODUCTION

While it's true that most parents experience great excitement when they bring home their "bundle of joy" from the hospital for the first time, it's also often true that a bit of anxiety usually sneaks in as the child draws near to the teen years. Remember when your parenting questions were things like: Will this child sleep through the night? Will I know when to feed this child? Will I know how to change a diaper properly? Will my little one have allergies? These seemed like such important questions when your child was young. Have your concerns become much more daunting now that your child is in his or her teen years? If so, you're not alone.

Many of the same parents who were so excited about their little "bundle of joy" now find themselves biting their fingernails when navigating through their child's teen years. Rest assured, a little help and encouragement can certainly bring back that same excitement. My hope in writing this book is that it will help you, as the parent of a teen, have a greater understanding of them as you discover what teens and Play-Doh have in common. Once you have this understanding, I believe you will see yourself as privileged that there is a teen in your house.

1

They Are Fun

No one can deny that Play-Doh is fun. The possibilities with Play-Doh are endless. It comes in many different colors, in cool looking cans, and it's fun to hold. You can smash it, roll it, shape it, create with it—the list goes on and on. But how does the thought "teens are fun" strike you? Are you as convinced that this is true? If you really think about it, it can be so true.

Think about it this way: Has your teen (or one you know) ever done something so dumb (in your opinion, not theirs) that you just had to stop and laugh out loud hysterically because of it? I know I have! Or have you ever asked your teen, "What were you thinking?" and their quick response was, "I don't know. It just looked fun!" It may not always feel like it, but teens are fun to have around the house because they can often be a good source of some serious laughter.

I'll never forget one such incident from my son's thirteenth birthday party. Since his birthday is in the summer, we often created some sort of treasure or scavenger hunt around our house for all his friends to enjoy. This particular year, the plan was that everyone would jump in the pool for the grand finale. However, the boys decided that jumping into our pool would not be as much fun as jumping into our canal. And so they did! The only problem with the canal was that alligators and monitor lizards lived in there. (Yes, we live in Florida!) Though they all thought they were just having fun, needless to say, it took me a little longer before I was as convinced. Let's just face the facts: if there's fun to be had, our teens want to be right in the middle of it. Sure, some of the things they do, say, or wear just make us want to crack up. Quite often, we can't help but wonder, "What are you thinking?"

All the teens I know are convinced that the most important thing in their lives right now is their "fun." Sure their fun may not fit into the exact mold of what we would call fun, but we are mature adults now. The fact is, if there is fun to be had, there is a teen somewhere lining up for it.

Think about it this way: Would your teen rather hang around his or her friends, or do chores around the house? Would your teen rather go to the movies or stay home and do homework? Would your teen rather be playing video games, heading to the mall, swimming at the lake...or just sitting around at Grandma's house? (No offense, Grandma!) Let's be honest. If they could choose, they would choose to be where the action is.

Whether we like it or not, teens believe that this season of life is all about them having fun. And if we aren't going to provide it, they'll find a way to create it themselves. This focus on fun is not a bad thing. In fact, it's quite normal.

The teen years are a time to be adventurous, to experience new things. Teens want to be given more freedom. They are trying to enjoy their lives in the midst of finding their own identity and wrestling with dramatic physical and emotional changes. Again, these things are normal. It's how we, as parents, help our teens navigate through these years that can make all the difference in the world.

Do You Remember When?

Do you remember what it was like to be a teenager? Some of the best times of my life were during my teen years. Sure, I have a few regrets (who doesn't have a few of those in life), but overall I have plenty of fun memories. Some of my greatest memories are of the slumber parties I went to, the high school football games I went to, and the summer camps I attended. I'm sure we can all remember some wonderful, fun days from our youth; after all, fun was often the "agenda."

No doubt we all put a few gray hairs on the heads of others during our teen years. This is why I'm so thankful for God's Word. I recall the psalmist telling the Lord, "Do not remember the sins of my youth and my rebellious ways..." (Psalm 25:7, NIV). If we read the verse just before this, we see, "Remember, Lord, your great mercy and love..." (Psalm 25:6, NIV). I can just imagine the psalmist worshipping the Lord one day, singing this amazing song of thanks to God, and then suddenly throwing in this thought, *Oh, and by the way, Lord, thanks for forgetting about all of the dumb, immature things I did back when I was a teenager. I sure do appreciate that you don't hold those things over our heads forever.* Think about it. Basically, that was what he was saying here.

Now, as much fun as the teen years are, they are also extremely valuable. Decisions are made during these years that can have lifelong effects, for good or bad. Unfortunately, most teens don't think about this along the way.

What's Happening in That Brain?

Believe it or not, studies prove that the brain of a teen is still developing. This explains a lot! The helpful news is that the part of the teen brain that is still developing is the very part that nurtures their decision-making process. Most people attribute bad decision-making in teens to raging hormones or immaturity, when it is actually the result of neurobiology.

Research proves that the frontal lobe of the brain is the part that develops last and can continue to change up into our early twenties. This area of the brain is responsible for reasoning and problem solving. The frontal lobe of the brain is the part that puts on the brakes (so to speak) when we are tempted to take risks or seek thrills. Are you beginning to see the picture here? The issue is not *what* they are thinking but *how* they are thinking. If this part of the brain is not yet fully developed, it is easier to understand some typical teen behaviors.

The bottom line of what I am saying is this: Be patient while your teen's brain continues to mature. It will take time for them to gain the ability to wisely answer questions, such as: "Is this really a good idea?" or "What are the consequences of me taking this action?" I am not saying teens cannot use this part of their brains at all (though some would love this excuse), I am simply pointing out that they are going to access it a little more slowly. It is also important to know that the brain of a teen (or child), is more excitable than the brain of an adult. Their brains are attuned to everything going on around them, which explains why they are always ready to join in on the fun. The upside of this is that they have a great ability to absorb and learn information.

Spreading Their Wings

If we are honest, we know that most teens just want to experience life to the fullest. (Remember, it's all about fun!) Teens are looking for adventure—new experiences. At the same time, they desperately want to fit in and find acceptance, especially among their peers. This, of course, is why they are often willing to take risks in order to have fun or to simply fit in. I consider this the time when they are trying to spread their wings of independence. This is something I encourage you to allow while they are still under your roof. Please understand that by this, I do not mean allowing foolish or destructive things.

Not long ago, our seventeen-year-old daughter came to us and asked if she could invite her "friend" over to have a chat with us. This "friend" happened to be a young man from our church who was a few years older than our daughter. Of course, my husband and I obliged. The young man shared that he "liked" our daughter and would like to have permission to "get to know her better." My husband, being the gracious father that he is, put his hands on the young man's shoulder and said: "You may like my daughter, but you may not date her at this time." We explained that we would gladly allow them time to build a friendship and allow them to see where it went from there.

Over the next few months, we allowed this young man to come over a couple nights a week and have dinner with us and build a friendship with our daughter, under our roof and under our watch. (We did our best not to smother them too badly.) During those months of "friendship," we continued to praise our daughter's actions and behavior and let her know that because of the way she was handling this situation, she was really earning our trust. She was so open and honest with us every step of the way. After a short period of time, they made the decision to just remain friends. We remain grateful for this opportunity to watch our daughter spread her wings and make some decisions without anyone getting hurt along the way.

The Mama Hen

I will openly admit that I am one of those extremely "motherly" mothers. Even in the youth ministry I lead, I have often been referred to as "Mama Hen." So this area of letting our kids spread their wings is a tough one for me. After some "wrestling matches" between my kids and I, I have learned how to allow them to spread their wings and have fun, as long as I know they will be safe. Through this, I have had plenty of opportunities to teach my teens how to make wise decisions in the midst of fun opportunities. This can be exciting and difficult at the same time.

The night our son turned eighteen, he was invited to a graduation party. His eighteenth birthday happened to fall on the last day of his senior year. He and his good friend assured me they would be fine going to this graduation party and that they would remain wise. Since our son had earned our trust over the years, we allowed him to go. After all, it was his final day of high school and his eighteenth birthday. And his goal, he shared, was to go and be a light to his unsaved friends.

I'll never forget our son's excitement when he returned home many hours later. He shared that upon his arrival at the party, many people said things like, "Comer, you're here?" and "Hey, Comer, what are you doing here?" welcoming him in, while other teens scurried off, trying to hide what they were doing.

You must understand that our son is a very friendly, fun-loving young man who was also known to be a sincere Christ-follower in his high school. He genuinely lived out what he said he believed. For this reason, he was respected by many of his peers. He told us excitedly that he was able to talk about Jesus with several students that night. Some of them even agreed to come to church. He was so proud of how God used him as a "light in the midst of darkness."

To be honest, when he first asked to go to that party, my first reaction was an emphatic "no." Then I got that look from my husband that reminded me that our son had earned our trust and it was time to let him spread his wings. Thanks be to God, it turned out even better than I expected.

Teens want to have fun and they want their parents to trust them. It is one thing when you let your kids start picking out their own clothes to wear or which games they want to play. It's another thing when you hand over the car keys and have to trust them to make wise choices while they are out, and then return when they are supposed to, all because they want to have a good time.

Ecclesiastes 12:1 says, "Remember your Creator in the days of your youth, before the days of trouble come and the years approach when you will say, 'I find no pleasure in them'" (NIV). The writer is telling young people not to allow the excitement of youth to cause them to forget their Creator.

I like to explain it this way: It's absolutely normal to have a zeal and excitement for life and a desire to have lots of fun; however, remember that the source of real joy comes from knowing our Creator. He needs to be the center of our lives and must lead us in the decisions that we make—fun and all. After all, He is the one who made us.

Ecclesiastes 11:9 says, "Young people, it's wonderful to be young! Enjoy every minute of it. Do everything you want to do; take it all in. But remember that you must give an account to God for everything you do" (NLT). Oh, if we could only get every teen to understand and live this way! After all, isn't this how it should be? Young people want to have fun in life—and they should—as long as they remember who it is that has given them life and to whom they will ultimately answer.

Are We Having Fun Yet?

In the midst of all this fun we're having, how do we parent through these exciting and valuable teen years? Glad you asked! (Here's where more Play-Doh comes in.)

You have to be wise in how you parent your teen. The key is giving them freedoms when they earn them—certainly not before. Just because everybody else is allowed to do it doesn't mean your teen should be. Your teen is not everybody else. Often parents give out freedoms way too soon. Then once the freedoms get abused, they start pulling them back in again.

Think about this in light of playing with Play-Doh. First, you allow your child to pull out one can of Play-Doh—let's say the yellow—and you see how they handle it. Once they are mature enough to handle that one color, you can add another one, then another, and then another. If you put all the colors before them at once, they may well be overwhelmed. With all of the choices before them, they just might start mixing everything all together. Then all you would have left is one big blob of mess! Who wants that? (This is not what you want for your Play-Doh and most certainly not what you want for your teen.) So when it comes to giving your son or daughter freedoms, be wise. Let your teen earn their freedoms. Don't just give them all at once. This is where so many parents make huge mistakes they later regret.

I have counseled many families over my years in ministry. I've discovered that many parents allow their children or teens to have things, do things, watch things, or even pursue certain relationships only to realize in hindsight that they gave these freedoms way too early. This usually happens because parents want their children or teens to be happy. The problem is, once you give freedoms, it's difficult to pull the reigns back on them, especially when you feel they are being taken advantage of. Once you try to take these freedoms away, you will most likely notice a change in your child's attitude and behavior. Unfortunately, this is often where rebellion comes in, which can put a tremendous strain on your relationship.

If your child or teen is allowed too many freedoms too early, then eventually you may see the bad fruit (negative results) of them. To be clear, some of these freedoms are: permission to watch whatever television shows or movies they want, play whatever video games they want, listen to whatever music they want, explore whatever internet sites they want, or have a relationship with whomever they want, whenever they want. The problem is that as soon as you see the first signs of wrong behavior, you will want to pull the plug on the freedoms. This is where frustration and confusion comes in for your teen, because you've gone about it backwards. They need to earn freedoms *before* they receive them.

When parents try to take back freedoms they've already given their teens, they will usually respond by expressing a rebellious attitude. After all, the teens have enjoyed being able to make many of their own decisions. They were happy to be in control. This is why it is so critical for you to allow your son or daughter only the freedoms they have proven they are mature enough to handle. There has to be absolute trust that they can handle the freedoms before they are given. When you see that your teen knows the difference between right and wrong, and that he or she can make wise choices, this is the point when you know you can trust them to make wise decisions and allow them more freedoms.

So how does all this tie in with fun? The goal for parenting your son or daughter should be, "Start children off on the way they should go, and even when they are old they will not turn from it" (Proverbs 22:6, NIV). Only as they mature over the years do you allow them more and more Play-Doh "color choices" or freedoms because you know they can handle it. These freedoms range from allowing them to dress themselves appropriately when they're younger, to deciding on which "fun" activities to participate in, even eventually hanging out with someone of the opposite sex. Remember, in this season of life, they just want to have fun! Just make sure that in the mix of their fun and making choices, they are first grounded in godly morals and values. This way, you can ensure the freedoms they are exploring are ones they can handle.

A Few "Fun" Instructions

The first time you hand your son or daughter a new set of Play-Doh, you give them a few instructions on how to handle it. Once instruction time is over, the fun begins. The Play-Doh is squeezed, shapes are made, and praise is given for what is created. So in order for fun to be had by all on your exciting journey of parenting a teen, I want to encourage you with a few instructions as you begin to do some squeezing, shaping, and molding of your own. Trust me, if you learn to do these things, it will make your parenting journey much more fun along the way!

- Instruction 1: *Teach them the truth of what is right and what is wrong, according to the Bible.* (I'll get more specific about this throughout the rest of this book.)

- Instruction 2: *Encourage them along the way.* Life-giving and encouraging words are needed and appreciated by everyone. As your son or daughter grows and matures, you should be their biggest cheerleader along the way!

- Instruction 3: *Celebrate what's right.* In other words, when your teen makes wise choices, whether big or small, praise them so they know they are going in the right direction.

- Instruction 4: *Pray.* Throughout your parenting years, prayer for God's wisdom is your greatest tool. Your hope is that eventually you will watch your son or daughter mature into a God-honoring adult. At this stage of the game, their adult years are right around the corner.

Another thing, I believe, that teens and Play-Doh have in common is they are both moldable. Molding Play-Doh can be quite fun, while molding a teen may not seem as fun. In fact, at times it may seem painful, but let me assure you, it will be worth it in the end! I believe we are off to a great start, and the fun is just beginning.

2

They Are Moldable

Teenagers are just like Play-Doh because they are moldable. And like Play-Doh, the possibilities are endless.

If I handed you a clump of Play-Doh right now, what is the first thing you would do with it? If you were like most people, you would give it a nice big squeeze. Not only would you *squeeze* it, smash it, and let it ooze out through your fingers, you would then probably try to mold it into something. I believe this is often what our teens feel we are trying to do to them—some squeezing, smashing and shaping. All the while, you are simply trying to mold them into something.

Did you know that teens feel stressed-out at times? Silly question, I know, but think about it closely. All teens experience stress, though they often handle it in different ways—and it's usually not a pretty picture. To be quite honest, they just don't always know how to handle stress very well.

Just like Play-Doh, teens can be stretched only so far before they start to fall apart. They experience stress from many pressures of life, including home, school, friends, and the list goes on.

A Walk in My Shoes

I am sure at least once in your life you have heard a teen say, "You just don't understand!" And if you are like most parents, you probably responded: "I was a teenager once too, you know!" The truth is, both statements are accurate. All adults were teens, but in all fairness to them, we don't know what it is like to literally walk in their shoes as a teen today.

I am certainly not saying that we are totally in the dark on the issues teens face today. Unless our heads have been stuck in a hole somewhere, we should be aware of what they face, at least to some degree. Middle school and high school today are totally different from what they were back in our day.

For me, one of my worst teen years was the eighth grade. I was thirteen and forced to do a lot of growing up that year.

My mom and biological father divorced before I turned one. For the next ten years, my mom did the best she could to take care of me as a single mom. But she remarried right before I started middle school, and we had to move to a new city about thirty minutes from where I had lived all my life. I also had to start eighth grade at another new school—a horror of horrors for an eighth-grader.

Talk about feeling like a fish out of water! Somehow, all the kids going to my new school already knew each other. And it seemed as if everyone was out to get me. I had already been through some big changes in my life over the previous few years. The social stress and challenges of that school year only multiplied my trauma.

In all honesty, I was never a troublemaker. I loved to make friends, loved to have fun, and loved to feel accepted. I always strove to brighten up a room. But the girls in this school were not okay with all this. They would literally wait in the bathroom to bully me. I can still vividly recall being threatened on the school bus, that I would be "killed on Monday." Once a group of kids claimed to have put a Quaalude in my milk at lunch to see what would happen to me. (I didn't even know what a Quaalude was!) Fortunately for me, I became friends with a girl I nicknamed "Bud." I have always been a small-framed person, but Chris (aka "Bud") was just the opposite. She intimidated anyone that even looked her way. For some reason, she quickly befriended me and became my bodyguard for the remainder of that school year. Thankfully, I made it out alive.

Nothing New Under the Sun

As horrible as that school year was for me, I can honestly tell you that I believe that the many pressures teens face are far greater today. I say this not only because I hear stories of the incredible dysfunction, drama, and troubles from teens all the time, but because of what I see. Everything under the sun is so much more out in the open now.

While it's true that there is nothing new under the sun, back when I was a kid there certainly was more of a fear of God and respect for authority than what I see today. Times have changed. That's why peer pressure for teens today feels extremely weighty to them. The values many of us grew up with are rarely seen. Look around today and you will see plenty of people who live with little restraint and a lack of concern for maintaining strong moral boundaries. Again, the Bible tells us there is nothing new under the sun, and I understand that. It's just that everything under the sun these days seems a bit more exposed and out for all to see.

I believe that the influence of culture and media play a huge part in causing our kids to grow up way too fast (something I will cover more thoroughly in another chapter). This is why it is vital for parents to take on their God-given responsibility to do the majority of influencing and molding in the lives of their sons and daughters.

Let me assure you again that teens are moldable; however, there is usually a bit of squeezing that comes before the molding can begin. School expectations are at an all-time high in most places. There are APs, IBs, SATs, ACTs, and much more. Even in the sports arena, things are different. Back in the day, sports were a recreational activity the whole family could enjoy. Now there are far higher expectations and demands piled onto students and athletes. The competition is fierce. We have parents and coaches getting into fistfights on the field and coaches screaming profanities at our teens when they underachieve or underperform. All of these are pressures that cause our teens to feel squeezed. This is why it is vital for parents to do the right kind of molding and shaping in the midst of all the surrounding pressures. The key role here for any parent is to teach their teen how to appropriately process and handle the stresses they face.

Let the Molding Begin

With Play-Doh, the squeezing usually happens before the molding and shaping begins. Once the Play-Doh has been squeezed for a while, the ideas come for molding it into a cool shape. It's actually the same thing with teens. When they feel squeezed, it is prime time for some great molding to take place, if done correctly and in love.

By molding I am simply referring to character building. Character building or molding is accomplished by showing teens how to grow and mature from every circumstance. My husband has always been able to share great insights with our kids by doing this. No matter what the circumstance, he is able to use it to remind our son and daughter that they always have the choice to allow it to make them bitter or make them better.

You can teach your son or daughter to use the pressures and circumstances of life to learn and grow, and shape their character for the better. Understand, however, that the idea of being molded, especially by you, may not be at the forefront of your son or daughter's brain. Still, this doesn't mean it shouldn't happen. And as strange as it may sound, "molding" your teen during stressful times is something that can happen quite naturally, when done correctly.

How to Mold a Teen

It is best to attempt to "mold" your teen during a time when there is no immediate conflict between you. In other words, if you've just reprimanded your son or daughter, or one of you just raised your voice to the other, it would not be the best time for a life lesson. If your teen is upset at something you've just shared, allow him or her some time and space to breathe. Allow your teen to share what's going on in their world when they are ready. Help them feel they can safely vent to you without fear—and without immediately being given answers and solutions. Although you may have all the answers, they do not always want you to just fix everything right away. Sometimes they just need you to listen. Then when the timing is right, you can share your thoughts and wise counsel regarding the very thing they are going through.

No Conflict Zone

It is important to say more about the necessity of molding in the "no conflict zone." Make sure to share your wise counsel or advice when you are not in the midst of an argument or screaming match. If you are in a heated discussion with your teen, it is probably not the best time to try to share your advice. (Trust me, it doesn't work.) They really won't be listening intently at that moment. Sure, they can hear you, but it doesn't mean they are listening!

Let them talk. Let them vent (respectfully, of course). Let them share their struggles and stresses with you when they are ready and willing. Make them feel valued and understood in this process too by truly listening. Trust me, if you don't listen, someone else will. If you want to be the one they lend their ear to, make sure you show them you care first and that you are willing to hear them out. You may think they are handling their situation in a very dramatic or irrational way, but let them process it first. Just as with Play-Doh, the "squeeze" is taking place. Once they are in your hands, then you can begin molding and shaping your teen. Remember that their issues, however big or small, matter a great deal to them. School, friends, family, peer pressure, insecurities—all these things make teens feel like they are being squeezed, from time to time. They can only take so much before they feel as if they will fall apart.

I am not suggesting that you allow your teen to rant and rave or throw a fit whenever he or she wants to—especially in a disrespectful tone toward you. I am simply suggesting that you give them a safe place to share what they are going through to build their trust in you so you get the opportunity to begin molding.

Put Yourself in Their Shoes

Can you remember what it was like when you were a teenager? (It wasn't that long ago!) Think about how willing or unwilling you were to listen to the advice of your parents back then. Though you may have all the answers, the key here is to remember that your teen may not always want to hear what you have to say right when you feel like sharing it. I hate to admit it, but I have blown this piece of advice myself on many occasions. I often kicked myself afterwards, realizing that my "wise counsel" had fallen on deaf ears because my "listener" wasn't in the right place emotionally or mentally to hear me. At different times over the years, both of my children have asked me to just let them talk before I tried to fix their situation or give my opinion on a matter. I admit, I've often had to bite my tongue, but I also admit that I have learned as much as they have during these times.

Sympathy versus Empathy

Your teen does not necessarily need your sympathy all the time, but they do need you to be aware of or sensitive to their feelings and thoughts. When the time is right for molding, say things like: "I know I'm not in your shoes right now, but I remember going through tough times when I was your age." By taking this empathetic position, it defuses their defenses. If you can do this when they are willing to listen, you can gain a place of influence many parents desperately want to have.

More Fun and Games

Have you ever played the game, Cranium? It happens to be a family favorite around the Comer household. Cranium comes with a lump of purple sculpting clay. Occasionally, a player is instructed to sculpt the clue on the card for their partner to guess. Whenever it is my turn to be the sculptor, I panic when the egg timer is flipped because I have never been confident in my sculpting abilities. On many of these occasions, I think to myself, "How on earth am I going to mold this clay into the right thing?" As the grains of sand continue to fall to the bottom of the timer, my brain and adrenaline go on overload as I try to think of a clever way to mold the clay into the right shape in order for my team to win. I stare at the egg timer anxiously, knowing I have only a short time to make the masterpiece that will help me achieve my goal. I am proud to say that often, in spite of my panic, when it is all said and done, I am able to create something that makes sense. Miraculously, whether I thought it was going to happen or not, my partner was able to see and understand what I was trying to sculpt. This is very much the way it is with our teens.

Parents often feel as if the egg timer has been flipped on the years their teens have left at home, and that time is running out. Many parents frantically watch as each grain of sand falls through the hourglass. If this is you, let me encourage you to cling to the hope that you will one day see the masterpiece that is being sculpted under your roof.

Who Am I?

Every teen is looking for identity. They are discovering who they are. They try to take the pulse of everyone with whom they come into contact, wondering constantly: *Do they like me? Am I okay? Do I look good enough?* Do not simply assume that your son or daughter feels confident with who they are, what they look like, or in how other people view them. These are values they are truly concerned about most of the time, which is why love and encouragement from you during these important molding years are critical.

It bears repeating: Teens are moldable. Do not be surprised if they do not come right out and tell you that they appreciate your wisdom or encouragement when you give it. (That wouldn't be cool!) Just because they don't tell you does not mean they don't appreciate it (or that they won't in the long run). Even if your teen is not one to open up very easily, don't give up. Instead, remain consistent. Some teens are very open with their parents, while others prefer to stay closed for a while. I understand this because I have one of each. Many times, I have sat with them around the dinner table and asked the simple question, "How was your day?" From one of my children I would get a step-by-step, blow-by-blow report of the day's happenings, while from my other child (a teen), I would receive a simple answer like, "It was fine." However, I can say confidently that my consistency over the years in letting them know I care has been a huge key in keeping the doors of communication wide open. Thankfully, I am now seeing the fruits of my labors. I have found that the older my kids get, and the more consistent I have been in my parenting, the more open communication has become with both of them.

The Open Door Policy

The key in keeping communication open between you and your teen is maintaining an open door policy. In other words, make sure your son or daughter knows that the opportunity for them to open up and talk is always there on your end. When these opportunities come, take full advantage of them. Your teen won't necessarily want you pushing open their door very often, but they will find comfort in knowing that your door is open when they are ready and willing to talk.

Another important secret to molding your teen is to speak their love language. A great book to read on this subject is, *The 5 Love Languages of Teenagers New Edition: The Secret to Loving Teens Effectively*, by Gary D. Chapman. In his book, you will discover how easy it is to tell when your teen wants to be loved. Parents often feel there is a language barrier between them and their teen. Discovering if your son or daughter thrives on words of affirmation, physical touch, quality time, acts of service or on receiving gifts may well help you express your love and affection in an effective way.

I truly believe that you, the parent, are the one who can influence your teen the most. This is why it is so important for you to give love and discipline to your teen in a way he or she will understand and receive best. To do so, you would be wise to learn how your son or daughter shows and receives love most naturally. For example, does he or she show and receive love most naturally by: Speaking or hearing encouraging words? Giving or receiving a hug? Washing the car or cleaning their room? Spending quality time with family and friends? Giving or receiving gifts? I can assure you, it makes a difference when you meet your child on their love turf. It is amazing what can happen.

Both of our kids thrive on encouraging words. At the same time, one of my children does not need a lot of personal touch and closeness while the other one craves it. Once we took the time to learn how our son and daughter receive love from us best, it made a huge difference in our communication with them and it made molding their hearts much easier.

Conflict-Free Molding

Sitting at the dinner table with your teen is a great way to have some conflict-free molding and sharing time. I have so enjoyed watching the expressions on our teens' faces when my husband and I sit around the dinner table and share some of our growing-up stories. I am always delighted to hear their laughter or questions after we share some of the pitfalls, temptations, struggles, and fears we experienced growing up. Some of the stories we have shared have really made our kids crack up, while others have shed light on some of the darkest times we had in our teen years. Of course, we are always wise in what we share with them, doing our best to make each story a teaching opportunity.

I truly believe that hearing from us in these conflict-free times does help them let down their guard and realize we have been through some of the same situations or struggles they have. It really does help us become accessible and human in their eyes. They may not say it, but I believe our teens genuinely want us to be real with them. This doesn't mean we should air all of our dirty laundry with them, however. Remember to be wise in choosing the stories you share from your past (and when to share them). Be sure to use each one as an opportunity for molding.

On the Right Path

When I think about Jesus Christ, I remember that He always met people right where they were, right in the middle of their sin, hurt, confusion, or fear. He met them right where they were and right when they needed Him. In His amazing way and with His amazing grace, He was able to help them recognize their need for change while gently leading them right back on the path they needed to be on. As a parent, you should be willing and able to do the very same thing with your son or daughter, pointing him or her in the right direction.

I love the verse that says, "Let us run with endurance the race God has set before us" (Hebrews 12:1, NLT).

Did you catch those last seven, important words? This verse encourages all of us to run the race that God has set before us. In other words, the race we are running—and the one our teens are running—should be the one that God has set before us. It should not be the race (or life) any of us think is right, but rather the one that God has marked out for us. This is why it is so important to always point your teen to God and His Word. The most valuable thing we can do as we are molding and shaping them is to point them to Him. Finding answers in God's Word for their troubles is truly a beautiful thing. I have humbly realized over the years that I may not always know the answer, but I know the One who does. Teach them to turn to God and His Word, because that is where truth is found.

If your teen knows and understands that many of the people in the Bible were teenagers when God used them, it just might change their view of turning to God and His Word when they face pressures in life. The Bible is filled with stories of real people with real struggles, just like all of us. This is why it is so important for you and your teen to remember what Isaiah tells us: "We are the clay, you are the potter" (Isaiah 64:8, NIV). So let God continue to mold you while you do your best to continue molding and shaping your teen into what He already sees as a masterpiece. Your son or daughter may grumble and complain about all the squeezing, molding, and shaping along the way, but who wouldn't? In fact, just count on this happening, but don't you ever give up. Keep molding because a masterpiece really is in there somewhere, and your perseverance will be worth it in the end.

3

They Change Colors When Blended

The next thing teens and Play-Doh have in common is that they change colors when they are blended. When there is blending, there is changing.

Changes happen every day. Some changes are planned, while others are not. Some changes happen over time, while others happen quite suddenly. So any time there is a change in a family dynamic, planned or not, things will look very different. A family dynamic can change dramatically due to a tragedy, divorce, death, a new marriage, a big move, adoption, and more. Whatever the reason for the change, it brings a very different look and feel to life for us, but especially for a teen.

After many years of ministering to teens and raising a couple of my own, I am convinced that more than any other season in life, it is during the teen years that we wrestle most with emotions due to family issues. I also believe it is very healthy for teens to wrestle with their family issues during these years, especially if there has been any type of big change, dysfunction, or tragedy in their lives. Trust me when I say that if they don't deal with these issues in a healthy way during the teen years, they will inevitably carry them into their future marriage or family life. I believe this is why there are so many struggling marriages and families today (unfortunately). Too many people do not deal wisely with the family issues of their childhood or adolescence, so they wind up carrying them into adulthood. Then, as often is the case, it makes parenting through the teen years a little uncomfortable or awkward.

Normal or Dysfunctional

I realize there are many "dysfunctional" families around, whether they live right next door to you or perhaps even under your very roof. If we are honest, we could look around and see that a "normal" family dynamic (a healthy home with a God-honoring mother and father who are happily married, with kids in tow) is not really the "norm" anymore. This is very unfortunate, but also very true.

The reality is that when things in a family dynamic get mixed up, changed around, or blended together—whether for the good or the bad—everything that was "normal" to your teen will look very different. Just as Play-Doh changes when you add different colors together, so the life of the teen changes when family dynamics shift. When circumstances change in the family dynamic, the perspective of everyone in the household changes too, but especially the teen's. The point to remember is that when families are blended and things look and feel very different, you must allow the teens in your household quality time to adjust. I am not insinuating that all changes in a family will cause things to go bad or get worse, I am just asserting they will be different. So if there is a teen in the family, they just need grace to adjust to the changes. It is just like creating a brand new color of Play-Doh that wasn't in the original box—it takes getting used to.

The Blending of the Play-Doh

Flash back with me to a time when you had a brand new Play-Doh set before you. Remember all the colorful little cans: the bright orange, blue, white, and yellow lids that represented the exact colors inside? If you were anything like me, you anxiously anticipated opening those brightly-colored cans filled with moldable clay that were just waiting to be shaped.

Even while having great fun making new creations with my Play-Doh, I can remember working meticulously to keep the colors separate. The goal at the end of play time was to return each bright color of clay to its matching can so that everything would stay just as it was supposed to. But then it happened. I returned from the kitchen after making a sandwich to find that someone had decided to make green Play-Doh by blending *my* yellow and *my* blue Play-Doh—without my permission! After being gone only a few minutes, I returned to find my entire Play-Doh world had been changed. The colors were blended and there was no way to get them back to the way they were. Who said I wanted green? I liked just having the blue and the yellow as they were. Sure, green was a cool new color, but I didn't ask for a new color. Perhaps the intention was not to anger me by making a new color; it may be the intention was just the opposite. But the fact still remained that the yellow and blue I had in front of me just minutes before was now very different and could never be the same again. The yellow and blue were gone forever. Now I had green.

The new addition of the green color may not be such a bad thing in the long run, but the realization that the blue and yellow were blended might be a lot to swallow at first. It would take some getting used to.

Does this relate to anything your family—and specifically your teen—has had to deal with? If so, the best thing you can do is try to understand their perspective and allow them plenty of time to process the changes in a safe and loving environment.

My New Green

I have a soft spot for young people who experience dysfunction or go through big changes in their family while growing up because I can totally relate. My biological father and mother were married in their teens and divorced before I turned one. My biological father was a severe alcoholic and drug addict for most of his forty-five years, and was in and out of my life up until I was about ten years old. Throughout the years, there were many things I saw and experienced that would definitely fall under the "dysfunctional" category. On the occasions when I did visit my father, I can remember being surrounded by many loud "party people" and lots of drugs and alcohol. Of course, at that time, it was quite normal to me.

When I was ten years old, my mother met the man she knew she would be with for the rest of her life. Once they got married, she asked my biological father to give me up for adoption so that my new stepdad could legally adopt me, effectively removing him from my life. To my surprise, my biological father said yes! To this day, I can still remember walking down the steps from my fifth-grade classroom and being told that I would soon have a brand new daddy—and have a brand new last name. From my perspective, everything in my world—even as dysfunctional as it had been—suddenly changed.

For a little while, it all seemed like an exciting new adventure—strange at times—but still an adventure. Even though my mom had only known my stepdad for a couple of months, she knew she had married a good man. But from my perspective, I had moved to a new house, moved to a new school, been given a brand new last name, got a new set of grandparents, and the list went on. For me, everything had changed—literally.

For the first time in our lives, my mom and I no longer had to live in a trailer park on the bad side of town. We were actually able to have somewhat of a "normal" family life. It was a brand new beginning, and the excitement continued when my two little sisters came along a couple years later.

Then it happened. I became a teenager.

Once my teen years rolled around, I began to struggle mightily with the reality of how my life had been. I really struggled with the fact that I had been totally rejected by my "real" father. I began to deal with emotions and questions that I had long stuffed down deep inside; perhaps issues that I never even knew were there before. Not that it was a horrible thing. It was bound to happen. In fact, it needed to.

Quite honestly, I wouldn't change a thing now, because I do believe that everything that happened to me in my life has made me the woman I am today. Fortunately for me, I surrendered my life to the Lord at age sixteen, and I will always be grateful for the journey He carried me through. It was definitely smack-dab in the middle of my teen years when I finally began to deal with all of the stuffed emotions in my life. It was also a time when I was the most moldable. As painful and lonely as it felt at times, it all became worth it when I began to use my life as a testimony to others of the redeeming grace of our amazing God.

Where Do We Go from Here?

No matter what a family dynamic is like, if there has been change or dysfunction, some emotional rollercoaster rides should be expected during the teen years. This is especially the case in any family circumstance outside of God's original design. Even if family circumstances have changed for the better, as mine did, things will feel blended and require a time of adjustment.

Even if the family change or situation arose a long time before, the teen years are usually when the questions and emotions of it get stirred up. Teens do not automatically accept things just because they are told to accept them. Family experts will tell you that no matter what the situation is—whether good or bad—in a changed or blended family situation, it usually takes three to six years for true cohesion and harmony to be attained.

Your teen needs to know that it is acceptable for them to ask tough questions about their past or present circumstances if and when they need to. Your son or daughter should know that it's okay to wonder and it's okay to hurt. Just let them know that it's what they do with the hurt that will matter in the long run. This is why it is vital that you, as the parent or stepparent, be open to discuss the tough questions to come. In fact, I would encourage you to welcome them. If you handle the tough questions wisely and maturely, the healing will come along much sooner than if you stay closed and seem bothered by them.

I believe that you can use anything in life—a new change, a crisis, a dysfunctional situation, or a blended family—as a teaching tool for life. It is a beautiful thing when a parent can be open with his or her teen, especially when it comes to family matters. Teenagers may come across as if they don't ever want to talk about these issues, but trust me, deep down inside, they really do. So, have an open ear and an open heart to sense the right time to have these important conversations. If they are not ready to talk when you are, just give them space. Perhaps there may be someone else they would be willing to talk to. This is certainly okay, too.

Over the years, I have counseled many teenagers who have been through tragedies or family breakups when they were younger. For some reason, they were able to stuff their emotions down for a long time. It may seem to have never bothered them in earlier years. Perhaps by God's great design, they were able to do this until they were mature enough to handle the process of dealing with them and ultimately healing. There is just something about the teen years that triggers them emotionally and mentally, and makes them yearn for answers. The comforting news is that this is perfectly normal and quite healthy.

I have often heard parents say that once their son or daughter reached the teen years, they took a hands-off approach. While I do not believe in being a smothering parent, I do not agree with a total hands-off approach. There are certainly times when teenagers need to be left alone in order to process things on their own. However, as a parent, I wouldn't stay far away for too long. The last thing you want for your teen is for them to become a loner or hermit. You also do not want them to stuff down or hide their emotions behind something else, either. If they have experienced any potentially harmful situation over the years (whether emotionally, physically, or mentally), be sure they know you want to know about it. If they choose not to talk to you about it, then make sure you help them find someone else they can talk to. Be sure this is someone you both trust, and make sure it is someone who can help your teen process his or her emotions in a healthy way.

A Time for Healing

Each year in our youth ministry, I devote an entire month to teach on family issues and parent-teen relationships. Some of the recent series were titled: "Home Is Where the Heartbreak Is," "Broken Bridges," and "Extreme Home Makeover." The titles may be different, but the goal is always the same: To help teens deal with hidden pains caused by family circumstances and allow a time of healing. By the end of all of these series, we have a night of ministry where I ask all the students who have had any type of hurt, pain, rejection, or dysfunction in their home or family to come forward for the leaders to pray with them. I am always amazed at the overwhelming response, year after year. I couldn't even begin to tell you about all the stories we have heard from the students who come up and spill their guts. The stories about abandonment, divorce, rejection from a parent they never knew, constant fighting with mom or dad, abuse, and more go on and on. Whether it is the quiet teen who never says much, the outgoing teen who is in everyone's business, or even the big, tough football player, they all share similar struggles of pain and hurt stemming from family struggles.

When I taught a family series, "Broken Bridges," I had one of my youth leaders build a broken bridge on the stage of our youth center. Each week, I taught while standing right on that broken bridge. At the end of the series, I had each student who was dealing with a past or present family struggle or hurt, write it down on a piece of paper. Then I invited them to come up and throw their folded or crumbled piece of paper onto the broken bridge and ask God to begin to heal their hearts in regard to the situation they wrote down. I shared with them that even though their situations may have felt like one big broken bridge to climb over, it didn't mean they couldn't get to the other side. I assured them that though it may seem difficult, lonely, or awkward at times, they could be overcomers. I reminded them that the Bible says, "Let us run with perseverance the race marked out for us, fixing our eyes on Jesus, the pioneer and perfecter of faith" (Hebrews 12:1-2, NIV). Who better to focus on than Jesus? If He could help Peter walk on water, certainly He could help them get across a broken bridge!

During the series, once again my heart was so blessed as I watched teen after teen come forward—tears rolling down their faces—in response to what they were dealing with and what was happening in their hearts. Many of the teens even shared that they had never really opened up about their feelings or family struggles before, that only then had they realized it was a good thing to do. I encouraged them to deal with their pain now rather than take it into adulthood and ultimately, to their future families.

I must admit, the best part of all this was, I got to watch a beautiful thing happen. I saw the amazing love of a compassionate Heavenly Father come and surround these teens and begin a wonderful work of healing in their hearts. When they know it is okay to hurt and wrestle with painful issues, they realize they don't have to keep it hidden in their hearts anymore. They realize it is okay to ask God to heal their hearts. And if anyone can heal a heart, it's certainly Him!

Better Sooner than Later

Recently, a woman in her late fifties walked up to me and asked if she could talk to me. In a few moments in a hallway, she shared a bit of her life story. With tears in her eyes, she shared how she had been totally rejected and neglected by both of her parents growing up. She admitted that she had never really dealt appropriately with the pain from her childhood. She realized that because she had kept all the pain from this stuffed inside for so many years, it had carried over into her adulthood and her marriage. As the tears continued to stream down her face, she opened up about the brokenness in her husband's life as well, and how he hid his pain through alcoholism, day after day. Throughout her younger years, she had never known to deal with the pain and rejection of her past. No one had ever told her it was okay to hurt; that it was okay to wonder why things in her life happened the way they did. No one told her that the pain from her circumstances wasn't her fault. No one told her in her earlier years how to be free.

The good news is, she now has a relationship with the Lord and is allowing Him to finally heal her heart after all these years. I am certainly grateful for this, but I can't help but wonder how much more peaceful her adult years could have been, had someone helped her navigate through all her emotions many years before.

It is for this very reason that I spend so much time encouraging teens to deal with their life issues. I truly believe that when they can open up and wrestle with their life issues in their teen years, they will go into their adulthood with a much healthier perspective. Don't be afraid to attempt to have your teen open up, especially if anything has changed in your family dynamics. If the family has been blended or changed in any way over the years, it's important to get your son or daughter's perspective. Get a read on how they are handling the changes in their lives, especially as they relate to issues with your family. It is so worth your time and effort, even if they play hard to get at first. It is important to emphasize here that even if you feel you have a "normal" family situation, you just might be surprised at the insecurities your teen may be feeling. So do not take anything for granted. Do whatever you can to keep healthy lines of communication open.

Lessons Learned from a Scar

I like to think of any painful circumstance as a potential scar, but I mean this in a good way. A scar is a mark left by the healing of injured tissue. Did you catch that? A scar is a mark left by the *healing* of injured tissue. Usually, when we think of a scar, we think of the actual, literal mark that is left on our body due to an injury, but a scar is actually a reminder of the healing that takes place after an injury occurs. The focus is NOT on the mark or even the injury. Instead, the focus is on the healing that happened where there had been an injury. I don't know about you, but this makes me smile. My husband has a huge scar on his head where he once had 187 stitches due to a bike accident he suffered back in his high school days. Besides a crazy scar and a miraculous story, the fact is that he is alive, his body healed, and he has a big scar to prove it.

I like to think of it like this: A scar is simply a reminder of the fact that things were different before the injury, but now something is brand new. Although the skin will never be the same—just as Play-Doh will never be the same once colors are blended, or families will never be the same once the dynamics change— the scar shows that something has been healed. Sure, it may take some time to heal, but rest assured, the healing does come. This is really good news.

4

They Pick Up What's Around Them

The fourth thing that teens and Play-Doh have in common is the fact that they pick up what's around them. Can you remember when your children were younger and their playtime with Play-Doh was over? How did you have them clean up all those little specks of Play-Doh left on the table, the floor, or on their clothes? You probably did the same thing I did. You taught them how to ball up the Play-Doh and start pounding it on top of the specks in order to pick them all up. It was certainly the easiest thing to do.

Unfortunately, the little Play-Doh specks were not the only things picked up during cleanup time. Most likely, they picked up the dirt you didn't even know was there, along with lint, dog hair, crumbs, and any other dirty little thing on the floor or table with which the Play-Doh came into contact. In this condition, the Play-Doh is certainly still usable; however, it just happens to be carrying a few extra little things it unintentionally picked up. This is very similar to what happens with our teens. Whether we like it or not, they pick up everything that's around them, intentionally or unintentionally.

I must warn you as you read further in this chapter, that people who know me well know my life motto is: No Compromise, No Excuses, No Regrets! So this subject is one that I happen to be very passionate about. This is not just because I am a mother, but also a youth pastor. The fact of the matter is that teens are affected by whatever and whoever is around them—whether *they* think so or not. Influences come in all shapes and sizes and include friends, trends, media, and the list goes on. I assure you; anything or anyone your son or daughter is constantly around will affect them.

I Just Like the Beat

Remember when you were growing up and your parents would tell you to shut off a particular type of music because they said it was "bad"? I sure can! I know many parents of the time ranted about how horrible a "type" of music was for their son or daughter. (Perhaps this was just during the '80s, my high school years, but I don't think so.) Of course, back then my response was typical of many teens in that scenario: "I'm not listening to the words; I just like the beat." Yeah, right! Who was I trying to kid?

It is time we honestly admit that the culture around our teens is powerful and has a tremendous influence on them. It has the power to shape their very way of thinking, whether good or bad, whether biblical or not. This is why it is so critical that parents understand how to deal with these influences and do the right thing in helping teens filter through it all. Remember, the ultimate goal is to encourage our teens and lead them in the right direction.

Consider the influence of media. When I was growing up, I watched a lot of television. Being raised by a single mom for the first ten years of my life, with no siblings to play with, I spent a lot of time being entertained by the television. Many of the thoughts and opinions I had about life, family and relationships were shaped by what I constantly saw and heard on TV. I don't believe everything I saw was totally harmful, but it wasn't harmless either. That said, I assure you that what was in front of my eyes and ears back then does not compare to the messages and images our kids are exposed to today. Back then, the concept of putting inappropriate or suggestive images on a television or movie screen was unheard of. For example, when the television show, *I Love Lucy* showed Lucy and Ricky's bedroom, it had two separate beds in it—even though they were married characters in the show. (I realize I don't need to explain to you just how "far" down the immoral path media has gone.) We simply must take time to keep a close eye on what and who is influencing our sons and daughters.

Ungodly Influences All Around

In today's culture, it is not difficult at all to look around and see plenty of ungodly influences. They are all around us. Far too many of the influences on our teens—television shows, movies, actors, musicians, and video games—promote indecency and ungodly lifestyles. Whether we like to admit it or not, our teens really do pick up what's around them. Let's not forget that the Bible tells us: "Satan, who is the god of this world, has blinded the minds of those who don't believe" (2 Corinthians 4:4, NLT). It is disheartening, I'm sure, to be reminded that there is an enemy of God who does his best to influence people to live indecently and proclaim a message that is in total opposition to godliness. But this is something we cannot ignore. So let me ask you: Who or what are the loudest voices influencing your son or daughter? What messages are shaping and influencing your teen? I can promise you, these influences are coming from the activities they participate in and the people they hang around most.

Who's Screaming the Loudest?

Have you ever come right out and asked your teen what they think about homosexuality? I'm sure this is not a daily discussion, but I challenge you to ask them the next time you're cleaning up after supper or casually hanging out with them. You just might be surprised at their response. While the Bible is very clear that God absolutely loves every single human being on the planet, it is also just as clear that homosexuality is not a lifestyle the Bible promotes as a godly lifestyle. God made man and God made woman. God also defined marriage between one man and one woman. So why is there so much confusion on this type of subject for our teens today? It is simply because some very loud voices and some very big influences in secular media are clearly screaming a very different message than what the Bible teaches. With our culture promoting a message very different from God's Word, it shouldn't surprise us that our teens are confused. This is why it is imperative that you see for yourself what God's Word says on this or any subject.

If God's Word is your source, you should do your best to wisely influence your son or daughter accordingly.

It is absolutely true that Jesus loves and accepts everyone; however, He does desire that we turn away from any lifestyle that is contrary to what the Bible says is right or honorable. The same is absolutely true for anyone in any lifestyle that is outside the standards of a God-honoring life. Whether it's a lifestyle of drug addiction, alcoholism, promiscuity, lying, cheating, self-mutilation, selfishness, greed, and many others, the Bible is clear that God's ways are so much better than ours. After all, He sent His Son into the world because He loved us so much, and He knew we weren't doing such a great job on this earth without Him.

Don't Assume

Please do not just assume your teen believes the same way you do, that he or she believes what the Bible teaches, or automatically has the same convictions as you. This is why it is so vital and healthy to have conversations with your teen to discern where their moral compass points. It is critical to have those awkward talks about sensitive subjects, because if you are not teaching them the truth, the culture just may be speaking into their lives more loudly than you are.

Along these same lines, how often do you bring up the subject of sex in your home—as in sex outside of the confines of marriage? In God's eyes, sex is a great gift, but it is a gift to be used only in the confines of a marriage between one husband and wife. Today's culture, however, is screaming a much different message and doing so very loudly—all the time. You can't turn on the television or the radio (unless it's Christian-oriented) without hearing or seeing something pertaining to sex. You can't even go through the grocery store line without seeing a magazine crammed with articles on the subject. Trust me, if you are not talking with your teens about sex, it doesn't mean they are not talking about it. Surely you know they are hearing about it everywhere else. Most likely, your teen is having conversations about sex with someone, and this someone just may be shaping the way they think. Why not step up and be the key influencer instead?

Let's be realistic here. Never mind what your teen sees in the hallways at school, at the football games on Friday nights, or on the home page of Facebook. I assure you, the wrong messages are constantly hitting them right in the face. Don't pretend it's not there, (not that you could even if you tried). Talk about it. Be open about it.

Again, I encourage you to discover what the Bible says about the subject of sex and then share this truth with your son or daughter. I know from personal experience with our own kids that the more open we are about discussing these things in a healthy environment, the more comfortable they are about sharing their thoughts and asking questions in order to see things in a more appropriate light.

More Talk About Sex

Our teens should know that sex is a great gift, given for the pleasure of a husband and wife within the confines of marriage only. I cannot stress enough how clear the Bible is that sex outside of marriage—sexual immorality of any kind—is sin. This is not because God is mean and doesn't want people to have fun, but simply because He knows what is best for us. And why wouldn't He know what's best? He created us, after all.

Think about this: How many television shows or movies do you allow in your home that glamorize sex outside of marriage? How many of the shows or movies being watched in your home are saturated with perverted or crude joking, or "suggestive content"? Do an honest assessment of the messages you allow in your home. Take some time to discover what the Bible teaches about sexual immorality and then talk about it as a family. (Some great Bible verses to look up and discuss with your teen are: 2 Timothy 2:22, 1 Thessalonians 4:3-7, 1 Corinthians 6:9-11, 1 Corinthians 6:13, 1 Corinthians 6:18, Galatians 5:19, Ephesians 5:3 and Colossians 3:5.)

If you've allowed "junk" media in your home, admit it, then ask God to forgive you, and then do something to change what you allow from this day forward. You would be ignorant to think junk media is no big deal or that it is not affecting your kids. Choose now to be a strong voice and godly influence in your home and in your teen's life.

If your teen confesses to have already "messed up" in this area of their life, share verses like James 5:16 or 2 Corinthians 5:17 to encourage them in the forgiveness that God offers. I realize that this is not necessarily an easy or comfortable conversation, but it is a necessary one. The bottom line is, it's time to be real. No parent should have his or her head in the sand and no parent should avoid being involved in their teen's life.

A New Standard

Perhaps it's time to set some new standards in your home. Make a new commitment to not allow TV shows or movies in your home that promote sex outside how God intended it—within the context of marriage. Please believe me when I say that what you are allowing in your home or allowing your son or daughter to watch or listen to is affecting them way more than you think. Trust me. By setting higher standards on the media you allow, you will be setting your son or daughter up with greater ability to resist temptations and make wise choices for the rest of their lives.

My husband and I decided a few things many years ago. While our kids were growing up, we did not want cable television in our home. Old fashioned, I know, but this was our choice and it paid off in the end. Another decision we made was that we did not allow computers (or TVs) in our children's bedrooms during their middle school and high school years. Why? Simply to protect them from stumbling on things that they didn't need to see or hear. It is our responsibility, as parents, to protect them and train them up in the way they should go. I have never had qualms about keeping our standards very high, nor should you.

As I said, none of us should have our heads in the sand. We cannot and should not ignore culture or what's around us. We also should not be afraid of it. We must simply keep our standards high in the midst of our culture. Media and culture should not be teaching our children or teens about the facts of life. Let's trust God and His Word to do this. At the same time, let's do our part as parents to speak the truth. Not in a legalistic way, but in a sincere way.

Forbidden Fruit

A while back, I taught a youth ministry series called "Forbidden Fruit." (This was totally appropriate during the *Twilight* saga.) I had seen a T-shirt displaying the *Twilight* movie motto, "Forbidden fruit always tastes the best." As a youth pastor, with that as a lead-in, there was no way I could pass up such a great opportunity! At the beginning of the series, I put together a questionnaire and asked students a few questions about sex, such as: Is sex okay outside of marriage? Will God forgive you if you have sex outside of marriage? What does God think about sex outside of marriage? I was intrigued by many of their perspectives. Some students knew the biblical answers, but many had no clue of God's standards (according to what the Bible teaches), or about His amazing forgiveness and grace. If they were never told the truth from a biblical perspective, how would they know it? Everything else around them tells them sex is okay as long as they are ready. Unfortunately, many parents tell their teens this same thing! If this has been your perspective, please search out the truth in the Bible. You'll be glad you did. You want to be the one who sets the standards in your home, so why not go to the greatest source of all time for your answers!

Along your parenting journey keep in mind that Hollywood and MTV (along with other voices in our culture) are doing a fine job influencing our kids and teens. They go to great lengths to get their message out, so why shouldn't we?

Don't misunderstand me here. I'm not suggesting it's evil to watch television. We have had many family nights over the years (and still do), cuddling on the couch to watch a movie or show we all enjoy. I'm also not suggesting we keep our teens in a bubble, either. What I am saying is that we need to be wise and aware and set godly standards on behalf of those we have the privilege to raise and influence.

Parental Guidance

Each year at Christmas, we go to visit my husband's parents in the mountains of Virginia. On a recent visit, we all decided to go to town to see a movie. We decided on a comedy with a PG-13 rating, assuming it would be a fun family movie for all of us to enjoy together, all three generations together (grandparents, parents and our "kids"). Let me just say, sandwiched between my in-laws and my teens, I found myself very uncomfortable during many of the scenes in this movie that was supposed to be appropriate for a thirteen year old. My youngest at the time was seventeen. And although she was certainly old enough for the "content," several parts of the movie were just downright perverted. If my in-laws had not bought the tickets, I would have left midway through it. I was totally conflicted the entire two hours. Come to find out, once the movie was over, my in-laws shared how they were feeling just as uncomfortable as the rest of us. Perhaps I sound like a broken record, but I cannot stress enough how important it is to be aware of what your teen is watching and listening to. You should not care that the rating says PG-13—you should know the content.

The good news is there are many great resources available for you and your teens to look at before spending a few hours or dollars on something you may later regret. Here are two:

- www.pluggedinonline.com (Great for movie reviews.)
- www.cpyu.org (The Center for Parent/Youth Understanding is a great resource for music and up-to-date culture facts.)

My advice is to train your teen to be wise in what or who they allow to influence them. Remember, they pick up what's around them, whether it be video games, computer games, websites, social networking sites, and more. Talk about and set standards and boundaries with your teen. Look at your teen's Facebook page or whatever social network they may be on. Notice I did not say you should not allow them to do these things. Just be wise. If your teen is on Facebook, be a "friend" on their page.

I often sit and peruse my friends on Facebook that are students in my youth ministry. I like to check in on them via their Facebook status or check out their latest photos. (They have all given me permission to do so by being my friend on Facebook.) I am the type of youth leader that does not have a problem being honest with the teens I minister to. If I see something questionable on their page, I do not embarrass them in any way, but I do ask questions and make encouraging "coaching" comments when I feel I need to.

Recently, I mentioned to one of the young men in VOX (the youth ministry I lead) that I saw a photo he posted on his Facebook page and it concerned me that he would post that type of photo. I was not mean or rude about it, I was just totally honest with him, speaking the truth in love. He thanked me and went right home and changed it. It was a great confirmation to me that teens really do want people speaking into their lives when they know they care about them. Too many parents just allow their teens to go with the flow and figure things out for themselves, once they reach a certain age. From my perspective, if you have the ability to be an influence for good in your teen's life, then why not do so while you have the chance (without smothering them).

At one of my parenting seminars, I put together a list of questions for each parent to fill out to see how well they really knew their teen. Some of the questions were simple: Who's your teen's best friend? What's their favorite pastime? Other questions were things like: What's your teen's favorite type of music? Favorite singer or band? Favorite song? Of course, some of the parents knew the answers right away, while others struggled to respond.

The LID Method

During the seminar, I played some of the top current music videos for the parents and printed off lyrics to the top ten pop culture songs of that week. It was interesting, watching the expressions of the parents when I showed the music videos or read the lyrics. Many of them admitted they had never taken the time to really look and listen. I saw light bulbs going off in their minds. Some of the songs I showed or read lyrics for were the very ones they had written down as their son or daughter's favorite songs. So much of the music that is popular with teens today is packed with perverted or downright wicked content. Even some of the more innocent sounding music is not so innocent once you check out the lyrics or watch the videos. As you can imagine, parents were suddenly seeing things from a totally different perspective.

I realize that music is a very controversial topic. Who doesn't love music? Music is a powerful thing. It moves us and helps us relate to things in our lives in ways that nothing else can. Music is a tool that fuels so much emotion in all of us. However, so much of it is not appropriate or edifying to listen to. Simply put, it is a means of great influence.

I have a little tool I suggest you use with your teens to train and teach them how to make wise choices when it comes to what they listen to or watch. This tool can be used with music, media and more. I call it the LID method, which I find quite appropriate, since we are talking about teens and Play-Doh.

So what is LID? LID is a simple method you can use to help you set boundaries for the influences your teen lets in and what you allow. Here's what it stands for:

L = LIFT THE LID
I = INSPECT WHAT'S INSIDE
D = DECIDE WHAT YOU'RE GOING TO DO WITH IT

Let me break this down.

L = Lift the Lid

To lift the lid simply means to take a peek and find out what is inside the package. In other words, teach your teen to "lift the lid" on anything that has the potential to influence them. When a child gets their first can of Play-Doh, the first thing they want to do is lift the lid to see what they have to play with. This is what needs to happen here.

When your son or daughter is faced with a decision, they should learn to take a moment to choose whether or not what they are about to do is really something worth considering. For example, when my daughter was asked by some school friends to go see a horror movie, she was quickly able to "lift the lid" and answer "no" because horror movies have never been something she chose to be entertained by. However, if she was invited to do something that interested her, and it wasn't an obvious decision, she would then know to do a little more inspecting.

I = Inspect What's Inside

Inspecting what's inside means to take a much closer look at the message behind the song, movie, television show, video game, etc. Find out what it is really all about. Investigate the message. Just as your child would dump out the Play-Doh and start checking out what it can do, they should do the same with anything in front of them. Encourage them to listen to or look closely at the message of a song or movie. It usually doesn't take too long to discern the message.

Your teen should take the time to carefully inspect the "ingredients" inside the "package" to discern whether or not they could be inappropriate or unwholesome in any way. For instance, if my teen asks to go see a movie, we ask him or her to take some time to "inspect" the content of the movie. If it is something that is in contradiction to our values, then that's where we would help them to make a wise decision. (The websites I mentioned earlier help greatly with this by providing a lot of useful information.)

D = Decide What You're Going To Do

Here's where it really matters. Once your teen has taken time to check out what is in front of them, they need to decide what to do with it. Is this influence uplifting, innocent, or challenging in a good way, or is it something that is totally contrary to the values or morals they live by? Once this question is answered, the decision needs to be made: What am I going to do with what I know about this? Obviously, the goal is to teach your teen how to make wise decisions in choosing what they allow to influence them, what they should listen to or watch, and when to simply turn away from some things.

> Simply put:
> L = Lift the lid—Peek inside and find out what it is in the package.
> I = Inspect what's inside—Take a closer look at the message. What is the message really about?
> D = Decide what you're going to do with it—Will you watch it? Listen to it? Participate in it? Or, will you walk away from it?

The Bittersweet Side of Friendships

One other great influence is your teen's friends. If you haven't already noticed, your teen's friends mean an awful lot to them. Sometimes, you may even get the feeling that what their friends think about them means a whole lot more than what you think. In fact, this is usually the case during this season of life. What we need to remind them is that often friendships come and go, but their family will still be there for them at the end of the day.

On many occasions, my own teens have heard me quote the verse that says "bad company corrupts good character" (1 Corinthians 15:33, NIV). That's because the Bible makes it very clear that the company and friends we keep will affect our behavior and our morals. I personally appreciate this verse and other scriptures like it that remind us that our closest companions should be those that fear the Lord. I have also heard people say: "Show me your friends and I'll show you your future." Am I saying that your teen should never be friends with other teens that don't have a personal relationship with Jesus Christ? No. Jesus taught us just the opposite. Jesus loved everyone and poured out His love and compassion on people who were not like Him at all. But remember, He was the influencer, not vice versa. It is very important for your teens to find friends that will challenge them to live by the values they know are right. Friends that are like "iron sharpening iron" are the best ones to hang around with on a regular basis.

You should not be afraid to ask questions about your son or daughter's friends. You should know their friends; you should know with whom your teen is hanging out. You should know where they are going when they leave your house. Be inquisitive about who they are hanging out with at school. Do not be afraid to ask questions. Be concerned. Be involved. Allow them to have their friends over. Help your teen learn how to choose their friends wisely. They may not always seem to be listening, but they are. Just be consistent with your encouragement, even when it seems to fall on deaf ears. Trust me, you will not regret standing your ground when it comes to knowing something about the friends your teen is hanging around.

Perhaps you feel convicted because you have not set safe boundaries for your teen. Perhaps you feel you have been far too lenient in what you have allowed your son or daughter to listen to or watch or participate in. Perhaps you are concerned now about some of the friendships or relationships you've allowed. If this is how you feel, this can be a good thing. By all means, do the right thing from here on out.

This does not mean you should go on a rant and start burning up everything in the house that is a "bad" influence, but instead, sit down and honestly let your teen know you are re-thinking some things. You may need to ask their forgiveness for allowing them to take part in things that you realize now were unwise. Explain to them why you want to make some changes and how you want to go about it.

Recently, I was talking about this subject with a group of friends. One of the moms with a sixteen-year-old son came to me afterwards and said she was realizing that over the last couple of years she had slowly let her guard down and allowed her son to listen to whatever music he wanted to on his iPod. It didn't take long before he began exhibiting a very poor attitude and some very destructive behavior. She began to understand that much of the influence on his choices was coming from the music he was listening to.

After sharing this with me, she went home that night and, with tears in her eyes, asked her son to forgive her. She explained her realization to him, that she had allowed this music into their home and apologized for her poor decision. She then shared with him that she wanted to help him choose better things to influence his life. To her surprise, he told her he would delete his iPod's music library and select new music. This is a great example of how much teens really do want and need our guidance.

Choose to make some important family decisions like this together. Whatever or however this makes sense for you and your household, do it while there is time. Remember, just like Play-Doh, teens really do pick up what is around them, whether good or bad. So, as much as you can help it, surround them with good influences.

5

They Dry Up When Left Alone

Did you ever forget to put your Play-Doh up after playing with it and leave it outside the container overnight? Chances are, if you are like me, you did. When your kids were younger, did they ever happen to leave out a lump of their Play-Doh overnight, only to discover that it did not stay pliable? We all know what happens to Play-Doh when it has been left out for any length of time. It dries up. In fact, it gets as hard as a rock! Something similar to this can happen to your teen. If they are left alone for too long, they can become less moldable, which is the last thing you want to happen.

You may be convinced that your teen does not crave time and attention from you, but the opposite is true. Let's be honest, trying to love or mold a "dried up" teen does not sound like a very exciting adventure. While I do believe your teen should be engaged in the process of maturing and learning to spread his or her wings, I also believe you shouldn't leave them alone to figure things out all by themselves. There is a reason they are still under your roof. Simply put, they still need your guidance and attention.

I am not suggesting you have to have your teen glued to your side. This definitely wouldn't be enjoyable for either of you. I am also not suggesting that you lock them in your house until they reach adulthood. However, I will say without a shadow of a doubt that throughout the teen years, you should definitely be an involved parent. You don't need to be a nosy parent, a bossy parent, or a nagging parent. You just need to be an involved parent.

Have Clear Boundaries

Don't tell them I told you this, but teens really do appreciate boundaries more than they will admit. Not only should you set high standards in your household, you should also set safe boundaries. In other words, you need to have rules and curfews—what I call boundaries—that they are expected to live by as long as they live under your roof. There is a saying often used in our home over the years: "We're the Comer family, and the Comers don't do that." Any time our kids were interested in doing something or participating in something that was opposite our family values or the boundaries we set, we would simply say, "We're the Comer family, and the Comers don't do that." As simple or silly as this may sound, over time, it helped our kids learn how to process a situation and ultimately make decisions based on our family values.

When your teen knows where the standards or boundaries are for your family, they will also know when they're inside or outside those boundaries. You really aren't doing them any favors by letting them watch what they want, listen to what they want, hang around with whomever they want, text however long they want, wear whatever they want, or even go wherever they want. As I've already shared, these freedoms shouldn't be extended to your teen until you know they are able to handle them. By all means, don't smother your teen or look over their shoulder on every single decision they make. They certainly need space to breathe. Just be intentional about having clear boundaries and be involved with their lives.

The secret to teaching teens how to make wise choices is by having clear boundaries for them to live within. You should not allow things just because other people do. You're not other people. You are the one responsible for your son or daughter; not those other people. Your teen may seem to scream on the outside when they are reminded of your rules and boundaries. That's quite common. But at the end of the day, it's actually comforting for them to know and understand what's expected of them and that they have a safe place to land at the end of each day.

Let Them Know How Much You Care

As much as it is greatly beneficial for you to be involved in your teen's life, it's also beneficial to know how and when to be involved. Have you ever heard someone say, "They don't care how much you know until they know how much you care?" This is very true of your teen. They don't want to be lectured all the time. They also don't want to constantly hear about everything they are not doing right. Your son or daughter wants and needs to know how much you genuinely care about what's going on in their lives. You definitely want to make time for heart to heart discussions with them. Just do it at the right time.

I am confident that you have great wisdom to share, and you should share it. Just let the motivation to share this wisdom or to set boundaries be from an overflow of your love and concern for your teen. Your son or daughter wants your love; he or she wants your attention. I also believe they want and need your protection. Believe me when I say they really do want you in their lives, even if they have a funny way of showing it.

If damage has been done to your relationship over the years, then have honest communication about those things, ask for forgiveness for any wrong you've done to them, and then work on making your relationship better from now on. We cannot change our past, but each of us can certainly make decisions that will make our future better and brighter. Remember, the goal is a pliable heart, not a dried-up one!

Timing Is Everything

May I remind you that it is not wise to try and have a serious discussion with your teen at a time that would be awkward or embarrassing for them? Correcting them in front of their friends will certainly not win you any favor. If you are trying to have a serious conversation with your teen, just remember that timing is everything. Conflict-free times are best.

I remember a particular time when my daughter and I had a disagreement. I kept trying to prove my point, knowing that I was right and she was wrong. My error was in trying to prove a serious point when her heart wasn't ready to hear what I had to say. I realized she could hear me, but she wasn't listening. I chose to stop what I was saying, apologized for pushing my point, and said we could talk about it a bit later. To my pleasant surprise, in just a short time, she came and found me and asked if we could finish the conversation. After having some time to process what we were trying to discuss, we both had time to regroup and had a much calmer and peaceful conversation as a result. That's what you want to happen. At the end of the day, you want the heart of your teen to be in the right place.

Let's Talk Discipline

Discipline is certainly not a pleasant word, but it is a great teaching tool. The Bible says: "God disciplines us for our good" (Hebrews 12:10, NIV). God shows His love to us at times through the consequences we face when we sin. It is the same for our own children. Your son or daughter still need age appropriate discipline, even through the teen years. Just make sure that the discipline or consequences fit the "crime." Grounding teens for appropriate amounts of time, temporarily suspending their privileges, and similar forms of discipline go a long way in this stage of life.

If your son or daughter has done something wrong, then consider what the right consequence should be. Then let them know what the consequence is and why they are being reprimanded. You don't want to scream their punishment to them, but you don't want to ignore a life lesson and excuse their wrong behavior, either. Feeling the weight of wrong behavior is good for them. In fact, it's good for all of us. Also, try to stay away from phrases like "Your never" or "You always" when you speak to them. Remember, you want to speak the truth, but you want to do it in love.

This is why the boundaries or rules for your family need to be very clear and very fair. If your son or daughter willfully steps outside the boundaries you have set in your house, then you can rightfully allow them to face the consequences of their actions. My husband has a famous saying that he shares with parents: "Under the roof, under the rule." As long as your children live under your roof, they need to respect the rules of your home. When you set boundaries and rules that are used to teach and protect your son or daughter, the end result is a very good thing.

Kindness Leads to Repentance

The Bible reminds us "God's kindness is intended to lead you to repentance" (Romans 2:4, NIV). In the Bible, there are many examples of God's people sinning against Him, and of Him then allowing them to face the consequences. At the same time, we see that God's intention the entire time was—and still is—to capture the heart of His kids. This should be our motivation as well. Keep this in mind any time you need to discipline your son or daughter, or allow them to experience the consequences of their wrong behavior.

Have you ever witnessed a parent loudly and dramatically disciplining their child in public? I have and I can assure you, it makes it awkward for everyone around. That's why I have always tried to do my best to discipline, when needed, more privately. I can remember one time, when my son was only five and my daughter was three, I took them with me to the grocery store. Halfway through the store, my son decided to have a total meltdown and was not behaving well in the least. I firmly let him know that his behavior was not okay with me and that when we got home, he would receive a spanking. (Yes, we believed in spanking during the earlier years of childrearing.) I continued my grocery shopping, doing the best I could with a defiant five-year old and his three-year-old little sister. By the time we got home and I had unloaded and put away all of the groceries, a half-hour had passed, and I had totally forgotten that my son was due for a spanking. I will never forget seeing my little boy come around the corner in the kitchen with his head hanging low. When I asked him what was wrong, he said, "Mommy, you forgot you were supposed to spank me when we got home." Honestly, I didn't know if I should laugh or cry. That moment proved to me that our children really do desire to be right in their hearts and in our eyes. They crave our love, our approval, and sometimes even proper correction. This is still true in the teen years.

When it comes to disciplining your teen, it is not appropriate to degrade them in front of other people. It is also never appropriate or wise to discipline your son or daughter in rage. The psalmist said, "Lord, do not rebuke me in your anger or discipline me in your wrath" (Psalm 38:1, NIV). We should be thankful the Lord doesn't rebuke us in His anger. Let's not rebuke our kids in our anger either.

Ephesians 6:4 (NIV) says, "Fathers do not exasperate your children." Discipline is one thing, and it needs to happen. To exasperate your son or daughter is another thing. The word *exasperate* literally means *to squeeze the hope out of someone*. You do want to mold your teen, but you definitely do not want to squeeze the hope out of them in the process. Please do not do this. You want open, healthy communication, not constant tension and frustration. So choose to discipline when it is necessary, with the appropriate consequence, and pray that the result is a lesson learned.

Consequences should follow disobedience or disrespect. When there is sin, there needs to be consequences. Just make sure the consequences are appropriate. The idea is to teach, train, and equip our kids for their future. Use wisdom in your parenting. Do not be so lenient that you are uninvolved, and do not be so legalistic that you drive them away. You should want to help your teen process the circumstances of life for as long as you can. Remember, they are still learning and maturing as long as they are under your roof, and they should not be left to just figure things out all by themselves. It is way too easy to follow along with what the world is doing. Remember, your teen will dry up if they are left alone! So be involved and keep safe boundaries for them, while you can.

A Father Hunger

The role of a father is huge in the family dynamic. Children that are raised in a home with a God-honoring, loving father and mother are very blessed. Homes in which both parents love the Lord, model a healthy marriage, and are involved in their son's and daughter's lives are usually the homes in which teens thrive. What a blessing it is if this is the case for your household. Unfortunately, however, we live in a society where this is not usually the case, and the problem of the absentee father looms large.

There are many single-parent homes, and often the single parents that run them are mothers. I realize this is not always the case, but it certainly is quite common. I believe that over the centuries, the enemy of our souls, the devil, has done a great job of tearing down the value of the family. In the words of Jesus, "The thief comes only to steal and kill and destroy" (John 10:10, NIV). Unfortunately, Satan has worked very hard to steal, kill and destroy the value of family. I believe this is why so many families today are fatherless, leaving many young boys and girls hurting from what I will call a "father hunger."

Everyone craves the love of a father. It is a desire that is real and deserves attention. The absence of a father's love in the home—whether physically or emotionally—causes a deep craving for approval, which is why so many teens struggle with great insecurity. This doesn't mean all hope is lost for children in fatherless homes, but it does remind us that there is a void in everyone's heart that only a father can fill. I certainly do applaud the many single mothers who are doing the best they can to stick by their sons and daughters every step of the way. If you are one of them and this is your situation, I encourage you to find comfort in God's Word, where you are reminded: "He defends the cause of the fatherless and the widow" (Deuteronomy 10:18, NIV). Our Heavenly Father is certainly able to fill any void or hunger in any heart, especially the father hunger.

Eating disorders, rebellious behavior, promiscuity, cutting, and other destructive behaviors are often related to a teen's feeling of worthlessness or rejection. If this is a reality for your son or daughter, I highly recommend you find a life-giving church home where the Gospel is preached, that has a dynamic youth ministry (if you're not already in one). It is a great gift when you can have other caring people speaking into the life of your son or daughter. The hope is that your teen will be around the right people and mentors who can encourage them during this important and fragile season of life.

For me personally, at the age of eighteen, I was finally able to allow the Lord to heal my heart of all the rejection and pain I had stuffed deep down inside after my biological father gave me up for adoption. I vividly remember being in a church service and my pastor praying over me. He shared that the Lord wanted to heal my heart of rejection. All I remember was weeping and weeping until finally I felt an incredible peace in my heart as I finally let go of the pain and bitterness from that rejection. I realized for the first time that God's desire was to fill my father hunger in a way that only He can do. I am forever grateful for this.

6

It's What's On the Inside That Matters Most

I am certain that a great amount of thought goes into the packaging of Play-Doh. After all, Play-Doh packaging is cool—quite colorful and cheerful. It makes the thought of playing with Play-Doh fun. There is something about the packaging that makes you pay attention to it. Along the same line of thinking, the next time you go into a mall, walk into the coolest store—the one all the teens are going into. You will most likely see life-size posters of cool looking people dressed in the coolest fashions, all over the place. And you will see a bunch of teens wanting to look just like what they see on those posters.

Teens desire to have cool looking packaging too. They want to know they look cool with their style and that they fit in. While it's fine to encourage your son or daughter to look their best and smell their best, you need to remind them that what is on the inside of the package is what matters most.

We teach them how to say their ABC's when they are little. We teach them how to ride their bikes. We are there for them when they lose their first teeth. We are there for them when they move away from their first friend. But what should we do when they feel ugly or insecure? When they feel hopeless? When they feel all alone in the world? How should we teach them how to handle such things?

Over the years, I have learned that teens really do want to know their Creator. They want to know God. They want to know they matter to Him and that there is a purpose for their life. I see the hunger in students week after week. They want to experience the presence of God. They want to hear His voice. They want to feel His love. It is a privilege for me to help the teens in my life to live passionately for the Lord, but it's even more important for you, as the parent, to fuel this desire in them. The best way for you to do this is by living for Him yourself, modeling His character.

One day you should have the privilege of watching your son or daughter move on and carry with them the legacy you've modeled throughout the years. This is why I say it is what is on the inside that matters most. We all want beautiful children. We all want successful children. We all want to see our kids live happily ever after. No matter what you desire for your son or daughter, the greatest thing you should desire for them is that they have a genuine relationship with the Lord, and that they live a life that honors Him.

Over the years, I've enjoyed asking my son and daughter what they have been reading in their Bibles. I ask them to share with me what God has been speaking to them. Sometimes they shared very openly about what they are reading or about what they feel God is doing in their lives. Of course, this is not always the case. There have been seasons where they would simply shrug their shoulders. Perhaps these were times of insecurity, plain laziness, or they were simply not in the mood to talk. Whatever the case may have been, both my husband and I always tried to take the right opportunities to encourage them on their journey. We always reminded them that what matters most is what is on the inside.

Encourage your son or daughter to spend time with the Lord in prayer. Encourage them to read the Bible and journal what God is speaking to them or what they feel they are learning from His Word. Discover their favorite flavor of music and encourage them to listen to Christian artists that play and sing that style. Do whatever you can to encourage your teen to grow in the most important relationship they can have—the one with their amazing God. My favorite psalm in the Bible is Psalm 139:1-16, because it is a great reminder that God takes a personal interest in us right from the start. I encourage you to sit down and read it with your teen. I believe it will bless you both.

Just remember that while you're on this parenting journey, there will most likely be some ups and downs. There will be days when your teen will feel like they can conquer every hill they face, and other days feel as if they are standing in the middle of an anthill and cannot escape. The best advice I can give you is to stay the course, stay consistent, and remain hopeful that your molding is making a difference. Also, allow your son or daughter to wrestle with their doubts. Do not let their times of doubt discourage you. Instead, let them fuel you to pray more often to the Lord, that He would keep your teen on the straight and narrow path.

In the book of Matthew, we see an interesting response from the disciples who had been following Jesus. He had died and was now in His resurrected body, appearing before them. The Bible says, "When they saw him, they worshiped him; but some doubted" (Matthew 28:17, NIV). There they were, seeing Jesus, worshiping Jesus, but a few of them doubted it was really Him. These young men were wrestling with doubts that He was really there and that He truly was who He said He was. If the disciples could wrestle with doubts even after seeing Him—literally with their very own eyes—it certainly is understandable that our teens will struggle with doubt from time to time. Find comfort in these words because even in the midst of the disciples' doubt, the Lord showed up.

I have always said that more than anything else in this world, I want my kids in Heaven with me one day, once we've passed through this life. I want to know without a shadow of a doubt that my kids will live forever and ever—for all eternity—with my husband and I in the presence of our amazing Savior. Nothing fuels me more than this. But as passionate as I am about this, I also realize that my children are two human beings who have to find Him all on their own. I will do all I know to do to create an atmosphere in our home that is a loving, accepting, and safe place where my kids can feel like rock stars or have bad days of wrestling with insecurities. All the while, I will do all I can to assure them of God's great love. Because, after all, having God's love on the inside is what matters most.

Conclusion

As I conclude this final chapter, I would like to leave you with some words from another favorite psalm of mine. I pray this serves as a reminder about the importance of teaching each generation the truth about God, His Word and His ways. May great joy and peace be with you and your family as you continue life's journey, and may you find God's grace during this season of shaping and molding your teen.

Psalm 78:1-8 (NLT)

O my people, listen to my instructions. Open your ears to what I am saying, for I will speak to you in a parable. I will teach you hidden lessons from our past—stories we have heard and known, stories our ancestors handed down to us. We will not hide these truths from our children; we will tell the next generation about the glorious deeds of the LORD, about his power and his mighty wonders. For he issued his laws to Jacob; he gave his instructions to Israel. He commanded our ancestors to teach them to their children, so the next generation might know them—even the children not yet born—and they in turn will teach their own children. So each generation should set its hope anew on God, not forgetting his glorious miracles and obeying his commands. Then they will not be like their ancestors—stubborn, rebellious, and unfaithful, refusing to give their hearts to God.

Final Words

So, what do teens and Play-Doh have in common? It's quite simple:

1. They are fun.
2. They are moldable.
3. They change colors when blended.
4. They pick up what is around them.
5. They dry up when left alone.
6. It's what's on the inside that matters most.

Now, go buy some Play-Doh and have great fun with the teen in your house!